'It has really helped me find internal belief'
Sam (age 17)

'A collection of all the stuff that school tries to knock out of you' Ethan (age 13)

'Lightened my spirits'
Olivia (15)

'WOWZA!' Natalie (age 13)

'A really cool book. And I'm not even a teenager. YET!' Jack (age 11)

'A happiness book for teenagers? Mmmm. Not sure.'
Oliver (age 15)

'A happiness book for teenagers. Oh, yes pleeeease!'
Oliver's mum (age 43)

'Jam-packed with stuff that will help me have a BRILLIANT life!'
Isla (age 15)

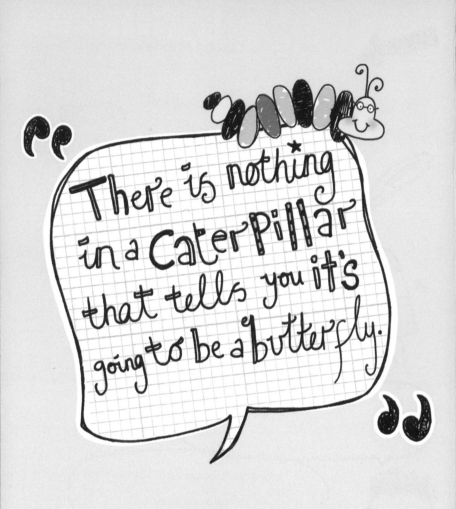

"There is nothing in a caterpillar that tells you it's going to be a butterfly.

Buckminster Fuller

THE ART OF BEING A
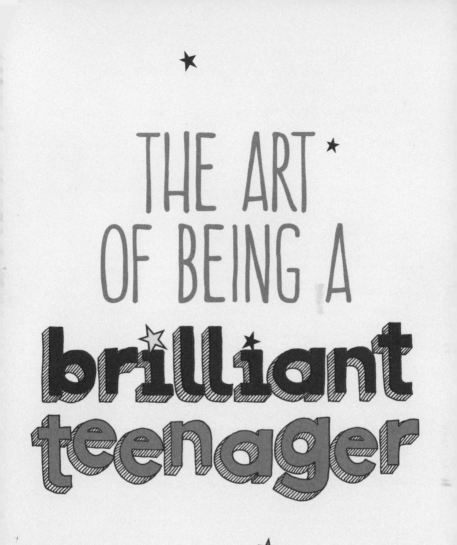

brilliant teenager

ANDY COPE, ANDY WHITTAKER, DARRELL WOODMAN AND AMY BRADLEY

CAPSTONE

A Wiley Brand

This edition first published 2015

© 2015 Andy Cope, Andy Whittaker, Darrell Woodman and Amy Bradley

Registered office

John Wiley and Sons Ltd, The Atrium, Southern Gate, Chichester, West Sussex, PO19 8SQ, United Kingdom

For details of our global editorial offices, for customer services and for information about how to apply for permission to reuse the copyright material in this book please see our website at www.wiley.com.

The right of the authors to be identified as the authors of this work has been asserted in accordance with the Copyright, Designs and Patents Act 1988.

Reprinted February 2016, November 2016, February 2017, July 2017, February 2018, May 2018, November 2018, January 2019, October 2019.

Library of Congress Cataloging-in-Publication Data is available

A catalogue record for this book is available from the British Library.

ISBN 978-0-857-08578-8 (pbk)   ISBN 978-0-857-08577-1 (ebk)
ISBN 978-0-857-08579-5 (ebk)   ISBN 978-0-857-08576-4 (ebk)
ISBN 978-0-857-08580-1 (ebk)

Cover design: Wiley

Set in 14/16.8 pt, Burst My Bubble by Aptara

Printed in Italy by Printer Trento S.r.l.

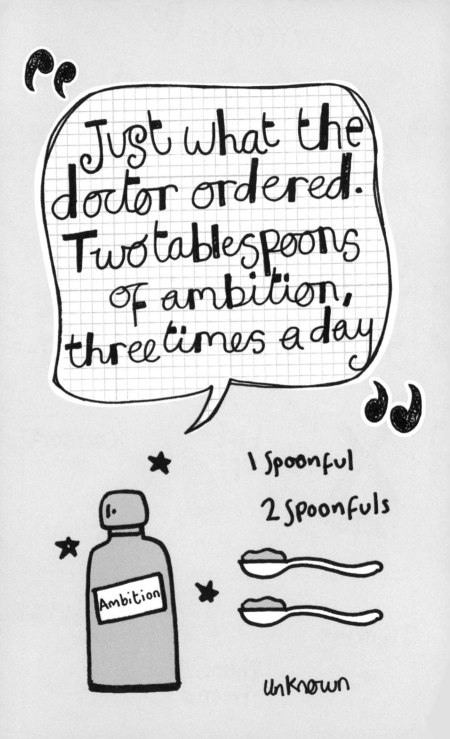

Contents

Foreword

Once upon a time I was sold a dream. I would grow up big and strong, get a fab job, marry the love of my life, have some beautiful children of my own and live happily ever after in a 5 bedroomed house, while I held down a job as a professional footballer or astronaut. It was going to happen. I just had to wait. Or, at least, that's what I was led to believe, when I was 7. And I was rubbish at waiting! I wanted to grow up. I wanted to be older. I wanted that fantastic future. NOW!

And my mum told me to slow down. 'Don't be in such a rush,' she would say. 'School days are the best days of your life.'

My parents must have been mistaken, right? They're old. So maybe their school days were different. Maybe they sat in one big classroom, where the older kids helped the younger kids. And it was pre-climate change when they skipped to school in their knickerbockers in the sunshine, swinging their satchels in glee. It was also pre-technology. Maybe they did their sums in chalk on black slates, and listened to stories passed down through the ages. And maybe their days consisted of weaving and carving, interspersed with singing shanty songs. And maybe this was pre-globalisation, when Britain ruled half the world and everyone had jobs.

And, before I knew it, I was leaving school. I started work and it was equally grim. I was paid but my money didn't last long. And whomever had invented the week had mistakenly divided it into 5 working days and only 2 days off. What's that all about? And relationships got even more complicated. And I wasn't an astronaut or a footballer. And the 5 bedroomed house turned out to be a single room here...

home
sweet
home

Where did it all go wrong?

This book is about making sure you avoid the mistakes we've made. We want you to have an extraordinary life. We want you to shine. We want you to achieve your ambitions, meet and marry your soulmate and get the job you always dreamed of. We want it to be Saturday morning inside your head every day. But, to achieve that, you need to be different from other people. Different in a good way. But, you see, the simple truth is

Shine

that it's easy to be yourself, averagely. It's easy to drift into a 'bog standard' life. That's why most people do! And, get this slightly painful realisation, it's more diffcult to be awesome. It takes a tad more effort to be your best self. It's an effort to be extraordinary.

And nobody's going to do it for you. Nobody's going to put that effort in on your behalf. Hopefully there may be people who can help, advise and support you on your journey to brilliance, but it's your life. And your responsibility.

There, we've said it! The terrible truth that teenagers hate. Being an extraordinary human being requires effort. The typical hard-wired reaction in most teenagers is to roll their eyes and sigh. 'That's so UNFAIR.' And this is as far as they'll get with our fabulous little book. They'll put this book down and return to their X-Box or reality TV or Facebook page. They'll be muttering, 'This book's not really for me. Average is easy. And *easy* is for me!'

But there will be a few who will be intrigued, especially at the vision of *'Saturday morning in your head'* because that's kind of cool. And they like the idea of being extra-ordinary. And they're aware, in the back of their minds somewhere, that they already have negative tendencies. They have already noticed themselves saying things like 'nightmare', or 'it's so unfair' or bragging about how rubbish they are at something. But they've figured that it's not too late to change these habits. And they're bright enough to understand that how you think will determine how you behave. And they've twigged that their behaviours will determine what happens to them. And, they've already grasped the most important point of all, that a bit of effort is well worthwhile.

So, if you've made it as far as this sentence, we reckon you'll make it as far as the end of the book. Maybe by the end of today? Because you know that the effort will be worthwhile. And you know that this book contains some gems that will nudge your life forward.

Welcome to the extraordinary world of YOU!

Getting Warmed Up

Warning! These words and messages are strictly for young people. If you're *not* a teenager please put this book down. *NOW*!

If you are a teenager, there's an 80% chance that someone bought this book for you. Most likely your mum or a well-meaning adult? If it's an e-book you will have downloaded it yourself because the adults don't know how.

In whatever format you are reading, welcome.

If an adult bought this book for you, *they* will be thinking one of the following things:

1. It will help you with your exams

2. It will help you feel better about yourself

3. It will help you focus more in class

4. It will help motivate you

5. It will give you the right attitude

6. It might stop you being an idiot

Do you know why they want all those things for you?

So *they* look good as parents!

All your parents and nan really want is to be able to tell other people how great you are.

'Oh my "whatever your name" is such an angel. They do this and this and this ... Blah Blah woof woof.'

Then they walk off with a smug look on their face, while the other parents feel rubbish.

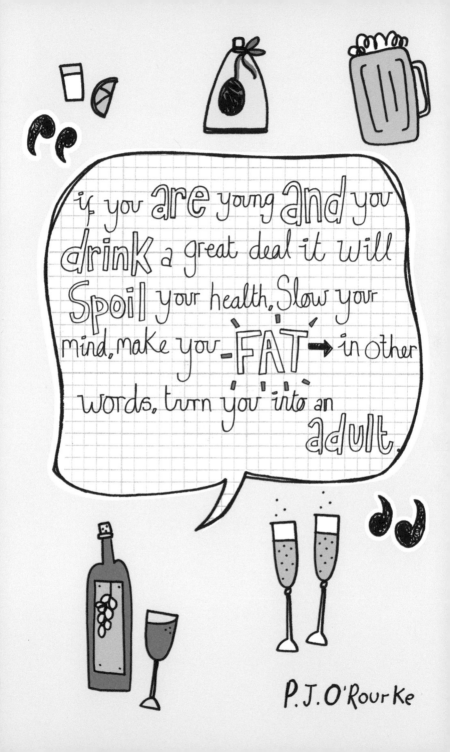

You won't understand this right now but the penny will drop when you have kids of your own. And that's quite likely to happen.

Lads, beware, it's easier to *become* a dad than be one.

soap on a rope

Shakespeare killed my love of reading. Grown-ups told me his stories were awesome. I thought they were rubbish and I didn't read a book for 20 years after leaving school.

This book is as far removed from Shakespeare as you can get. Your English teacher will think this book is awful. At least, that's what we hope.

This book will help you ...

Keep out of jail (Not a good place. Nasty things happen in jail when you drop the soap)

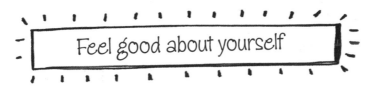

Feel good about yourself

Help you understand who you are – essentially an awesome human being (even though you do act like an idiot at times)

Give you the mindset of a champion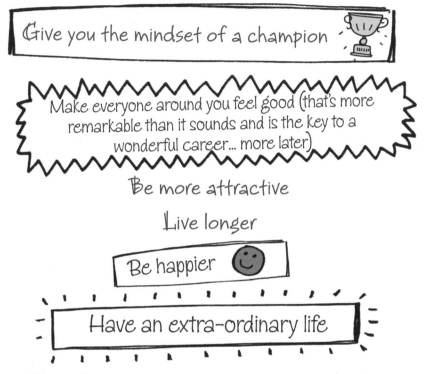

Make everyone around you feel good (that's more remarkable than it sounds and is the key to a wonderful career... more later)

Be more attractive

Live longer

Be happier

Have an extra-ordinary life

We couldn't give a monkey's about you reading other books or whether you tidy your room. We are not your parents.

we couldn't give a .....

These are the things we care about. We want you to:

1. Be happy

2. Find your way in this world and, ultimately, take the world by storm

3. Have friends you can rely on

4. Have a job you adore (one that doesn't feel like 'work')

5. Find a wonderful partner

6. Find your passion

7. Feel loved and awesome

The likelihood is that you don't know us and we don't know you. But, believe it when we tell you we care. And I mean we *really care*. The chances are we care more about you than you care about *you*. And we know that if you do what it says in this book, your life will be awesome. So it would really help if you cared too. If you don't give a s✶✶t about your future then there's not very much we can do.

But just so you're aware, life is a short and precious gift.

HOUStON, We have a Problem

The information in this book is based on a fundamental principle of one of the world's greatest philosophers ... Whitney Houston. She was a famous singer from way back, who said,

'I believe the children are our future.'

You probably think all famous people are happy. Whitney had all sorts of problems, caused by fame and money. She had an unfortunate incident in a bath and that was the end of her.

We wholeheartedly agree with Whitney's sentence. You are our future. But you might have noticed that a lot of older people whinge about 'the yoof of today'. Chill. Don't take it personally. They're probably just jealous. And they probably moan about just about everything else as well.

We don't moan. We think you are a bubbling cauldron

Of potential that can explode at any time (steady lads, you'll go blind).

Here's a painful truth. Not everyone fulfils their full potential. In fact very few do. Most people waste it, living their life in black and white. This book will allow you to live in full HD 3D Technicolour glory. No shades required.

But it's your choice.

Charles Darwin (famous bloke, Google him) came up with the idea of evolution, which means we, as a race, are improving and evolving all the time.

Learning is the future

You don't need to be particularly clever (although it helps if you are) but you do need to be good at learning. Learning to learn is the new superhero superpower. Pants on the outside? Optional.

Some teenagers are a bit more primitive than others. Beware the estates where there is a lot of sports' wear and not much sport. And never go in a pub with a flat roof.

Most people have the same insecurities. Everyone is afraid of being found out.

All parents want their children to be better than them. And all parents care — yes, even the ones who don't seem to give a s✭✭t.

We want you to be better than us. The world doesn't want you to muddle through. It needs you to come alive and, if you do, you'll stand out a mile. Most adults are a million miles away from feeling as great as they could. It's easy to end up like 'most adults'. It's a doddle to be yourself, averagely.

There's a town in Scotland called 'Dull'. And it was recently twinned with a town in America called 'Boring'. These towns may be small but, metaphorically, millions of people live there. You probably won't get that straight away because it's a really clever way of saying that most people get stuck in a rut.

The difference between a 'rut' and a 'grave' is merely the depth. Beware of both. They're easy to get into and hard to get out of. Especially the grave.

You're a long time dead. So make the most of being alive. Be *properly* alive. The average lifespan is 4000 weeks. That might seem a lot. But, chances are, you've already wasted loads of them being yourself, averagely?

Let's not waste any more.

Chemicals

Before we can move forward though we need to take a step back. You were created when your mum and dad had sex. If you feel the need to puke please do so, but come straight back. This is important.

When you were a tiny dot, inside your mum's tummy, you were a girl. All tiny humans come from female templates. Hairy-arsed lads, get over it. For some lads, this might explain something? It's why boys have nipples. When you are a 6-week old foetus, you get marinated in a cocktail of hormones that makes you into a boy or girl.

Males and females are supposed to be equal. There are laws that make it so. But girls might be a little bit superior? We suspect?

After 9 months of splashing around in amniotic fluid, you enter the world and someone slaps your arse. *Nice one!* And that more or less sets the tone. You have, from birth, been programmed to be cautious and have a negative attitude.[1] And while many things you have done in life have been your fault, this is not one of them.

It's your parents, family and teachers' fault!

You arrive with only two emotions, love and fear of loud noises. When you were a baby, was it too much to ask for a cuddle and the volume on the telly to be turned down?

Everything else including guilt, jealousy, anxiety, worry, and the popular teenager feeling of 'I can't be arsed' you have learnt from the people around you.

Mums and Dads are great at teaching you negative emotions, especially guilt. I heard in a supermarket yesterday a Mum say to her 3 year old daughter, 'Now Lilly, if you loved mummy you wouldn't do that would you?' Poor Lilly only picked up some sweets. I'm pretty sure that, later in life, Lilly will need some sort of counselling.

Guess what the first word is that most parents teach their kids?

[1] *We haven't got space to explain why. Email me if you want to know.*

'Mummy'? 'Daddy'?

Wrong it's, **'NO'!**

'No, don't do that darling.'

'No, stop climbing on the furniture.'

'No, stop pulling the dog's tail.'

'No, get your hand out of the fire.' (although if your hand is in a fire right now, do get it out)

'No, No, No, No, No.'

It's no wonder you can't be arsed doing anything - you have spent your life so far being told not to.

Instead, you are told to 'Sit there and be quiet' or 'speak when you're spoken to' or 'get your textbook out and turn to page 153'.

Most modern teenagers struggle to sit quietly and speak only when they're spoken to. You're desperate to interact with the world. When told to sit quietly, quite a few teenagers have a face like they've got a lemon stuck up their bum. Which is why they grunt a lot.

And grunt you should because the world has been out to get you from birth. A lot of young people complain that things aren't fair. I can't recall anybody ever saying life was supposed to be fair? Whatever it is that *isn't fair*, get over it.

They won't teach you this in physics but it's one of the rules of the universe. The harder you work, the luckier you'll get.

Remember, people will judge you by your actions, not your intentions. You may have a heart of gold – but so does a hard-boiled egg.

Anonymous

We don't care where you are in the teenage pecking order. Everyone can improve. Although it might be too late for us old folks (generic term for anyone over 27). You still have plenty of time to make a difference, not only in your life, but to the world.

Read the book, go back and read it again and then put it into practice. We guarantee you a better life!

The Glow worm Song
(unknown)

Being ♥ Real

It might sound a little sickly but this book is for your heart of hearts, for the voice inside your head and for the person you want to be. But, more than anything, it's for the person you already are. It is a reminder that you are already brilliant, sometimes. And that you need to start being brilliant a bit more often.

This book is also about reminding you to surround yourself with those who will replenish your reserves of energy, love and gratitude. Not the miserable b✸✸✸✸✸✸s who drain you.

"I ordered a wake-up call the other day. The phone rang and a womans voice said, 'What the **hell** are you doing with your life?'"

Demetri Martin
(American funny guy)

When we run 'The Art of Being Brilliant' in schools there is always a sizeable population of lads who want to be Premiership footballers. We admire ambition. I asked one such lad, 'So, are you any good at football? Do you play for a team?'

'Err no, sir. But I'm good on FIFA.'

You couldn't make it up. He reckons that if he stays locked in his bedroom playing on his X-Box for long enough, a Liverpool scout's going to knock on his door, walk in and say, 'Good with your thumbs. You're exactly what we're looking for. Here's a shirt and 200k a week.'

Ambition is fab. But don't delude yourself.

If you want to be a footballer you will have to be out practising 7 days a week and will have to be the star of your local team. Now!

If you want to be a vet, you need to be volunteering at the RSPCA. Now!

If you want to be a hairdresser, you need to be volunteering at your local salon. Now!

If you want to be in the army you need to be in the cadets. Now!

If you want to be a web designer you need to be designing websites. Now!

Tell me when you've got the point...

If you want to go to uni, you need to be working your backside off. Now!

If you want to be a banker you need to get used to having no mates. Now and FOREVER![2]

[2] Sorry, that's a cheap and topical gag. It might not be topical if you're reading this in 2050? But check out the history books. Bankers paid themselves lavishly while doing their jobs really badly and bringing the world to its knees. Top tip - try not to bear grudges #greedyb★★★★★★s.

People often say that a person 'has not yet found themselves'. But the 'self' isn't something you find, it's something you create. *Create* your best self and be it consistently.

You cannot give what you don't have. It's difficult to be nice to others if you're not nice to yourself. And it's diifficult to be nice to yourself when you don't feel good about yourself. Working on yourself and cultivating your own self-esteem can be a lot of work. In fact we believe it's a full-time job. And you never get a certificate of completion!

The longer you wait for your future the shorter it will be.

There's a really cool book called 'The Secret' that's based on 'The Law of Attraction'. Stick it on your birthday list. Put simply, what goes around comes around. If people don't understand you, take steps to understand them first. If people aren't nice, try being nice to them first. We promise that if you're consistently awesome, the world is a better place. It's a bit spooky how true this is.

Please note, it doesn't mean everybody is always nice and smiley and kind to you. The world will still have its fair share of idiots. Always remember, you can't cure 'stupid'. Just make sure you don't become one of the idiots. Do what it says in this book and, over time, you'll shine. And, when you shine, you stand out. And when you stand out, opportunities come your way.

We think standing out for all the right reasons is one of the most important things you'll ever learn to do. The problem is ... it's a whole lot easier to fit in! If everyone else is moaning about teachers and homework and that life's not fair, the easiest thing is to join in. Roll your eyes, sigh and complain. Try it. It's a doddle. Because doing what everyone else is doing is kind of tempting?

So, yes, fitting in is an OK short-term strategy. But your best long-term strategy should be to stand out. And if you're an upbeat, positive, smiley, energetic, enthusiastic young person, believe me when I tell you, you'll stand out a mile!

You get to choose your friends Choose carefully. It's better to have a few really good ones than lots of acquaintances.

Gangs are interesting. The media tends to talk about them as if they are a new phenomenon. We've been in gangs or clans since we emerged from the swamps. Gangs can make you feel like you belong to something. The problem is they tend to hang around doing bad stuff. We dare you to join a gang that does good stuff.

wanna be in Our gang?

Scouts is a gang. Drama group is a gang. Your rugby team is a gang. Netball is a gang. Playing in a band is a gang. Family is a gang.

Do stuff. All the kids who get into trouble are the ones that are bored. We appreciate that doing stuff takes effort. And, of course, it's a lot easier to do very little.

You don't get to choose your family. Make the most of what you've been given. They're for life. A family is only ever as happy as their least happy child. So make sure it's not you. You can be a source of pleasure, pride and inspiration to your family. Or a real pain and a worry. Think about it. If changes are necessary, don't wait. Make them.

bonus Story

MELANIE

When I was in primary school my teacher sat me next to a girl called Melanie. Or 'Mel'. And Mel was really nice but in year 3 she developed a scowl and a bad attitude. She adopted a catch-phrase that reflected exactly what she thought of school. Mel would slouch very low in her seat, roll her eyes and complain that everything was 'Booooring'.

And I mean 'everything'.

In year 3 we were taking turns reading pages from a story. I loved the story but when it was Mel's turn she sighed and huffed, 'What's the point of this story miss? It's boooring.'

In year 4 we did maths. It was never my strong point but I did my very best. Mel stuck her hand in the air. 'Miss. What are we doing this for. It's just numbers and they're really booooooring.'

Year 5 was especially bad. 'Miss, why are we doing history, it's just about dead people and it's **boooring**.'

Ditto year 6. Then it was the step up to big school. You've guessed it, Mel slouched her way through years 7, 8, 9, 10 and 11 complaining that big school was exactly the same as little school. '**Booooring**.'

Mel found her niche. She nestled into 'just below average'. Her default attitude was negative. Her exam results reflected her personality. And I couldn't help feeling that Mel might have wasted an opportunity?

bonus activity

This is an absolute corker but it requires you to be brave. Very brave indeed! Yikes!

Think of someone you admire. Maybe someone who has supported you or looked after you or has sacrificed their time and effort to bringing you up. Someone who inspires you, makes you feel good and whom you respect.

Write them a letter of gratitude. Write from the heart. What have they done for you? How have they helped you? How do they make you feel? What would you like to say to them?

Write at least a page. If they're in the same house as you, find them and read it to them. If they're not in the same house, phone them and read it. We dare you!

Email us and tell us how it went

you are you

We're born completely and utterly flawed. You pop out into the world, open your lungs and the starting pistol of life signals that you're off...

You are you. You just don't know it yet! And, eventually, you get used to being you. You work out what works and doesn't work for you. You suss the system.

Now I don't want to get too deep too quickly but have you ever stopped to consider which bit is 'you'?

Is it the body bit? Grab your ear lobe and feel the smoothness of it. The little hairs. That's a bit of 'you', right? Or bite your lip. Ouch, that's definitely 'you'. Pull your hair. That's attached (unless you've got extensions in which case you'd probably best not pull it too hard)

My cells

so that's 'you' too. There's a physical 'you'. That version of 'you' that's basically a bunch of trillions of cells stuck together. And the physical 'you' is very important.

But this book is less about the 'you' that you see when you stand naked in front of the mirror. Yes, yes, we know there are a load of lumps, bumps and imperfections. But herein lies the clue to you #2. Who's the one noticing your reflection? Who's the one saying, 'I wish my boobs were bigger' or 'I wish my moobs were smaller'?

We reckon this is the real you. The lumpy, visible bunch of cells is just the mechanism you use to transport yourself around. The one in your head is the most important. The one that feels and connects. Some call it your spirit, or personality or inner voice.

If I ask you, 'Do you talk to yourself?' The real you is the one who says, 'I don't know, do I?' And that's the version of 'you' that we want to engage. The one inside. Because if we can get through to the real you, our job is done.

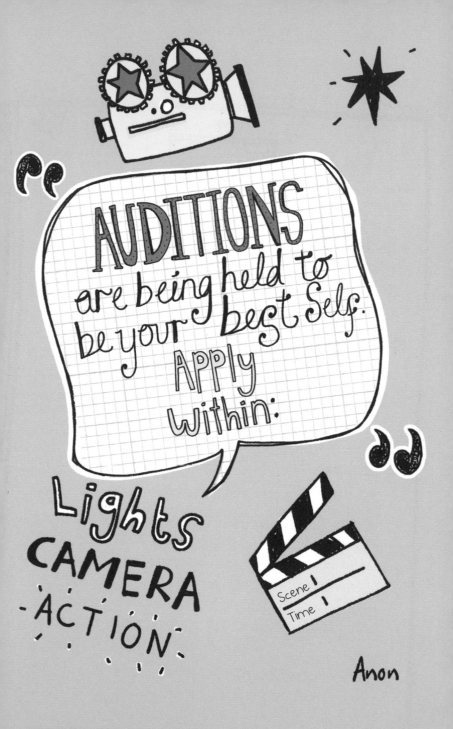

Here's something to think about. It might be a metaphor or it could just be a story about dirty pants?

A young couple moved into a swanky apartment in a new neighbourhood. They sat in their kitchen having breakfast, watching the world go by. The woman saw her neighbour pegging out the washing. 'That laundry's not very clean,' she tutted. 'She either needs a new washing machine or better washing powder.'

Other than the crunching on his toast, her husband remained silent.

His wife's comment was exactly the same the next day. And the next. 'Why on earth is that woman hanging out dirty washing?' she sighed in disgust. 'She needs lessons in basic hygiene!'

And her husband crunched, knowingly.

On the fourth day his wife plonked herself at the breakfast table with a gleeful smile. 'At last,' she said, pointing at their neighbour's washing line. Her husband followed her gaze to the neatly arranged clothes line where the whites sparkled and the colours shone. 'All of a sudden she seems to have learned to clean properly.'

And her husband broke his silence. 'I got up early this morning and cleaned our windows.'

If you thought this was just a cool story, then that's fine. If you realised it was actually about you and the way you view the world, then that's even finer. We all look at life through a lens. We are very quick to judge people. What if a better approach was to change the way you look at things. Clean your own lens. Viewing the world more optimistically and positively will almost always get you a better result.

We like this written by one of our heroes, David Taylor:

This week on Monday and Tuesday, really go for it. Be your true self and unleash your true and total personality on the world. Take action, enjoy life to the full, see the very best in everything and everybody, and help others to do the same. Surround yourself with positive people (this will happen automatically, because when other people can do something themselves, or believe they can, they want to tell you that you can too), smile when you see the sun, laugh when you feel happy, bubble with love, energy and the thrill of being alive.

On the Wednesday and Thursday, go for nothing. Be that impostor who inhabits your thoughts and body, do nothing, complain a lot and say that life has got it in for you, bring others down by telling them how you feel. Surround yourself with negative people (this will happen automatically, because when other people can't do something themselves, or believe they can't, they want to tell you that you can't either). Frown when you see the sun, cry when you feel sad, freeze with fear and the nightmare of existence.

And on the Friday ask yourself this single question - which of these two days did I enjoy more?

If it was the Monday and Tuesday - live like that every day.

If it was the Wednesday and Thursday - live like that every day.

In modern terminology, we think this is a no-brainer. Make your choice.

Habits

Positive habits are like a financial investment. Do them now, and regularly, and they'll give you automatic returns later. Habits are simply things that we repeatedly do. Your brain is elastic. Scientists would call it 'neuroplasticity'. This means your brain is a marvellous piece of kit that is always learning and changing.

Often, at the habit forming stage, will-power is not enough. Let's take regular exercise as an example. It's a battle. There's hassle involved. Rather than fighting the habit we believe you must change the habit. And that involves changing your underlying thinking.

We know we want more out of life than TV and Facebook. I got sick to death of getting out of things because I couldn't be bothered. That's why I ended up sitting in front of the TV vegging out on fast food meals.

It's easier to watch TV than write your novel.

It's easier to play computer games than get stuck into doing your homework.

It's easier to stay in bed for an extra half hour than get up and exercise.

It's easier to moan about the weather than stick your wellies on and go jump in some puddles.

It's easier to watch a talent show on TV than learn to play the guitar.

It's easier to watch Jamie Oliver and then go and buy some fast-food, than cook your own.

It's easier to fit in with the mediocre masses than stand out as a modern day superhero.

It's easier to stay in bed until midday than get on with achieving your ambitions.

Basically we're inherently lazy buggers, drawn to things that are easy and convenient. And unfortunately, being self-critical and sinking into negative conversations is easier than shining brightly.

You are a walking powder keg of potential change. You can change at any moment.

You can change your knickers. You can change your library book. You can change your brand of yoghurt. You can change your friends. You can change your mind, your hair, your mood or your habits. We readily acknowledge that some of these changes are easier than others.

It's comforting to know that your brilliant self is always inside you, sort of bubbling under the surface. It gets covered over with stuff you think you know. You accumulate layers. You learn how to be. You want to fit in and be 'normal' so you do what everyone else does.

That's the game folks. Please don't play it.

Chasing Rainbows

Groundhog Day, what a great movie. Even if you haven't seen it you'll be familiar with the phrase. As a teenager once said, slouching into one of our school sessions, 'Same s✱✱✱, different day.'

And she's kind of right. Life can become a little bit... samey? We call it 'having a C+ life'. Everything's just kind of 'OK'. In school report terms you 'could do better'.

On being left in a parking lot for 500 million years...

'The first ten million years were the worst' said Marvin, 'and the second ten million years, they were the worst too. The third ten million years I did'nt enjoy at all. After that I went into a decline'

Marvin the paranoid android, Douglas Adams, The Restaurant at the End of the Universe.

Lots of teenagers worry. And worrying about stuff uses up mental bandwidth. Famously, Einstein didn't know his own phone number. He carried it around on a piece of paper because he didn't want to clutter his brain. Homer Simpson is the same. He told Marge he wouldn't go to night school because every time he learns something new it pushes some old stuff out of his brain.

Both Einstein and Homer are wrong. Your brain has plenty of capacity. Don't worry about it filling up (there's that word again!). The trick is to fill your brain with the right stuff.

Your brain is often likened to a computer. One comparison we do like is that your brain has a spam filter. It selects the crap and dumps it before it gets to your conscious awareness. Which is fab so long as we trust the spam filter to block out the bad stuff and only allow in the good stuff.

Just for a second, imagine if your computer's spam filter worked in the opposite way and it blocked all the wonderful emails that said what a great person you are. It deleted all the good stuff and brought only bad news, stress and misery to your attention.

Sadly, that's how most people's neurological spam filters work.

Worrying is in your genes. It's the same with all creatures. Let's take mice as an example. Famously, it's always the second mouse that gets the cheese. The positive, confident, happy-go-lucky mouse was a victim of its own enthusiasm and never got round to passing its genes on! The bar on the mouse trap comes down with one hell of a thwack.

In a similar fashion, it's your most cautious ancestors that survived. If we open our minds and go with Darwin's theory, we're descended from creatures that roamed during the ice age.

We had positive and happy ancestors that, when the sun peeped out thought, *'Ooh, nice sunny day. And I bet it's going to be nice again tomorrow. Let's have a bit of a celebratory do.'* And they got crushed by the ice.

Those who survived were cautious. *'It's a nice day today so I'll work extra hard in case it's not nice again tomorrow.'* So for the happy ones who partied like there was no tomorrow, there was no tomorrow. The cautious ones stored some food. Hence, it was their genes that were passed down.

To us!

Brace yourself. This is

MASSIVE.

'Happiness' has been sold to you as a fantastic pot of emotional gold, buried at the end of the rainbow. It's a wonderful feeling that you want more of and it's 'over there'. Happiness has been mis-sold as the reward, the elusive end point that we all crave. It's something you must earn, or pursue.

And the mis-selling scandal begins when you're very young. Your parents and teachers tell you that if you work hard at primary school you'll get great SATs results. And when you get those great results, guess what? Then you'll be happy.

And they will have told you that if you work hard at big school you'll get some As and A*s and then you'll be happy. Am I right? Or am I right?

And you'll get a job and you'll have a sales target. And when you hit your sales target, then you'll be happy. Or you'll be happy when you're walking down the aisle with your perfect partner.

You are sold the vision of 'I'll be happy when ...'

In terms of tweaking your thinking, what if that's a big fat lie? You need to claim compensation from whomever sold you this vision of happiness. What if 'happiness' is a fantastic feeling - a pot of emotional gold at the end of the rainbow - but what if it's at our end?

What if being happy NOW is the key to success? It's the X-marks-the-spot on the treasure map of life.

marks
the spot

For example, what if it's the happiest kids that get the best results? What if it's the happiest, most upbeat sales person that naturally gets on with people and generates the most sales, month after month. What if being happy now is the key to finding your perfect partner because, let's face it, you're much more attractive when you're smiling.

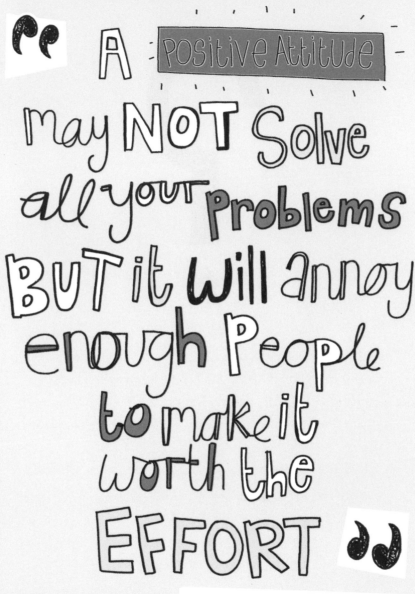

"A POSITIVE ATTITUDE may NOT solve all your problems BUT it will annoy enough people to make it worth the EFFORT"

Herm Albright
(German Guy, GOOD painter)

And this line of inquiry leads me to a very big question, one that's already been hinted at in earlier chapters - what if we've been looking for happiness in the wrong place?

A lot of the religious, philosophical and academic literature points to NOW as being the best (and only) place to be happy.

Holy cow! Now? Wow! But how?

Monkey Magic

How do you catch a baby monkey? Sounds like the start of a joke but, read on, this is true.

First, to catch a baby monkey, you have to go to a place where monkeys live (i.e. the jungle) and dig a hole in the ground. You then fit a cage into the hole and place a piece of fruit in the cage. Whoever sets the trap then retreats behind a tree and waits. Said primate will scamper through the forest, see the fruit and think, 'Yum yum, I like fruit'. Our furry friend will then reach in and grab the prize. But the cage has been designed so that the primate can't get the fruit through the bars.

Picture one bamboozled baboon, confused chimp or muddled macaque - its arm is in the cage, fruit grasped tightly - but it's unable to get the food into its mouth. The monkey-catcher doesn't have to creep out, really quietly, and pounce on the animal. He or she can simply saunter up to the puzzled primate, as loud as you like, and capture it. 'Gotcha! Lifetime in Zoo for you.' The creature can see the man approaching and knows it's going to get caught. Yikes! All it has to do is let go of the fruit and do a runner. But, here's the rub, the monkey would rather hang on to the fruit and get caught.

Which, once again, leads us onto a really interesting metaphorical question - how many bananas do we have in our heads? How many negative thoughts do you continue to think - thoughts that aren't serving you well but you continue to think them anyway:

'I'm rubbish at so-and-so.'

'I'm sooo stupid.'

'I'm too inexperienced to go for that job.'

'I'm not confident enough.'

'I'm not clever enough.'

'I'm stuck.'

'I'll never be good at maths/English/PE/art/history/etc.

'He'll never go out with me.'

'She'll never go out with me.'

Or behaviours? Things that you actually continue to do even though you know they're doing you no good:

Watching too much trashy TV.

Eating too much junk food.

Having an extra 15 minutes in bed rather than doing any exercise.

Walking with slumped shoulders instead of having a spring in your step.

When someone asks how you are, you reply, 'Not too bad, considering.'

Just as in the monkey story, we all need to let go! Here's a startling realisation … the biggest thing stopping you being brilliant is YOU!

Of course, it's almost impossible to let go of a belief you don't know you have. That sentence sounds odd, but beliefs are so ingrained that, often, they've become such a part of you, so entrenched, that you're not aware you've made them up. So, highlighting what your metaphorical bananas actually are and thinking them through is actually a great starting point.

Think about it. What do you keep saying or doing that is holding you back?

Drop the bananas!

PASSION
BRAND: YOU

Think of the stuff you buy. You will be drawn towards certain brands and away from others. Think of the coolest brands you know. What makes them cool? Why do they stand out?

I'm guessing they stand out in your head for positive reasons?

No matter what you think, when people hear your name they conjure up some thoughts and feelings.

You are a brand. Do you stand out for the right reasons?

What do you have to do to be a brand that shouts 'positive', 'cutting edge', 'original', 'revolutionary' or 'pretty damn sexy'.

It's very in vogue to have a tattoo, a piercing or to have your private parts waxed. Be careful, they all involve pain. For some reason that we haven't quite fathomed, girls pluck their eyebrows off and then pencil them back on? Some people have the fat removed from their thighs and injected into their lips? Apparently some people bleach their bum hairs too? Just saying.

Bum **HAIR** Bleach

If we said 'don't do those things' then we'd sound old. So we'd better not. We understand that looking good makes you feel good. And we want you to feel good. Just a gentle reminder, looks are skin deep. Please don't do 'shallow'.

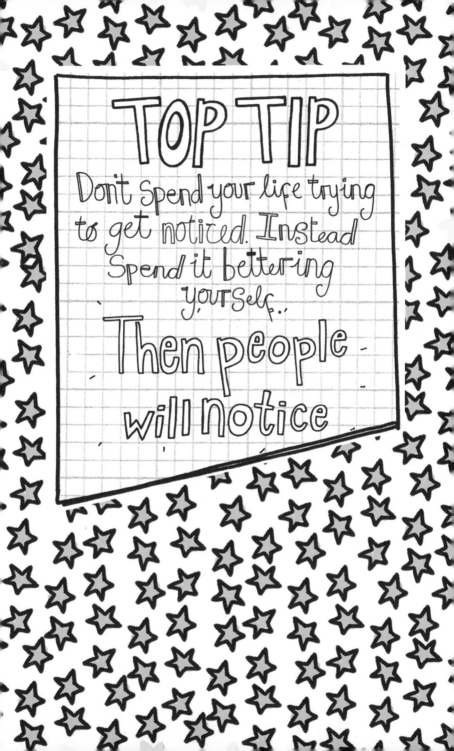

The sexiest thing you can wear is a smile. Everything else we've written is true but this is the truest.

Proof? I saw a bright orange teenage girl hobbling along in high heels, pencilled eyebrows, pumped up boobs, dyed hair (with extensions), manicured nails and (I'm guessing) glittery nether-regions. It must have taken her 3 hours to get made up. And she had a scowl on her face that could curdle milk. Yikes! Why bother? She'd be much better off unmade-up, but confident and smiling.

Besides, one day (when you're a bit older, we hope) you will sleep with someone and maybe spend the night. Which means you will wake up next to that person. I promise you, you want to wake up with the person you went to bed with. Life's too short for too many hasty exits.

Listen up, this is crucial. You have to find your passion. I wanted to finish the book now because, to be honest, if you find your passion everything else just fits into place. I also wanted to finish it at this point because I'm also a bit lazy.

You were born for a reason. Don't listen to anyone else, including your parents, if they tell you otherwise.

We think Simon Sinek's diagram below is pretty cool.

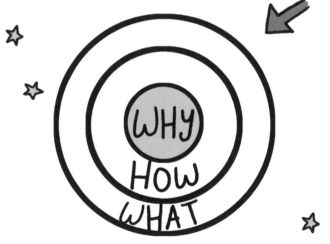

It can be applied to school, work or life.

Let's have a go with 'school'. Most young people start at the outside of the diagram and work inwards. And most people are fine with the 'what' and 'how' bits.

For example, if I asked *what* lessons do you do at school?' You'd be able to answer me, most probably with something like:

'Science, maths, English and stuff.'

'And *how* do you do those lessons?'

'Erm, I sit and listen, mostly. Sometimes we do science experiments and in PE we run around a bit.'

The crucial and often missing bit is the *why?* If I asked you '*why* are you learning those subjects?' you might struggle before offering something lame such as 'because I have to' or 'to get some GCSEs'.

We think you need to start with your 'why?' In fact, we think that if you can get your 'why?' sorted, the 'how?' and 'what?' will look after themselves
So, here goes.

'*Why* are you going to school?'

'Because getting the best education I can is crucial to me

making the most of my potential. School is a massive opportunity, handed to me on a plate, and I want to make the best of it.'

'*How* do you do that?'

'I do that by turning up to every lesson in "learning mode". Yes, even the boring lessons really matter because they show that I'm capable of sticking to tasks and getting on with people.'

'*What* subjects are you studying?'

'Subjects that will set me up for life.'

Shazam! You've found your 'why?' and your rocket ship is ready to launch!

If your parents moan about their job and how tough the world is, take note and learn from it. Or maybe they moan about not having a job?

Either way, they're half right. Life can be tough, but only if you haven't found your passion. If you are doing what you love, work isn't work at all. Not many people achieve this. (But we have, which makes us worth listening to.)

Listen to moaners (there are plenty out there), but don't ever become one. The truth is they haven't found their passion. It's as simple as that and has nothing to do with the economy, the government or anything else they may grumble about. Yes, we know that it rains a lot. But that's not an excuse for having a bad life!

Find your passion and then hang around with people who have found theirs.

If you want to better yourself, hang around with people who are better than you. If you want to worsen yourself, hang around with people who are worse than you.

If you want to feel attractive, get an ugly mate. If you want to feel rich, get a poor mate. If you want to feel confident, get yourself a shy mate. And, in the modern world, everybody needs a gay mate.

Don't look at glossy mags and wish you were that person. Only compare yourself to yourself. Being yourself brilliantly is the key to happiness and success. Every morning, look at yourself in the mirror and ask yourself, 'How am I going to be brilliant today?' and 'What am I going to do to make my teachers, parents, gran and friends go "WOW!" today?'

Then do what you just said.

Or here's a

cool lil game...

Imagine there's a version of you sitting up on a cloud. Go to the window and give yourself a wave. 'Hi to me, sitting up so high. It sure looks comfy up there!'

And that version of you is looking at your life. The on-high you is watching the down-to-earth you

as you go about your day. What advice would the sitting-on-a-cloud self give your real self? What would they say about the attitude that serves you best? How would they advise you to behave? How would they say you should treat teachers, parents, friends, brothers & sisters? How much effort would the on-high version of yourself tell the down-to-earth self to put in?

We'd say follow that advice because it's the best you'll ever get.

Are you improving as a person every day?

There's a saying ... the grass is always greener on the other side. Translated, this means life always looks better 'over there somewhere'. Here's something you won't get until you're much older, but we'll tell you anyway. 'Over there' isn't any better than 'over here'. Yes, the grass may look lush, but to stretch the metaphor a little too far, the key is to become a better gardener. Grow the grass around you. Appreciate what you already have. List 10 things you really appreciate but take for granted:

1.

2,

3.

4.

5,

6.

7.

8.

9.

10.

Holy mackerel, you're lucky! Look at what you've already got!

Happiness is a big fat 'X-marks-the-spot'. The reason why most people don't see the 'X' is because they're standing on it. Happiness is right here, right now (that's a massive concept. Don't worry if you haven't a Scooby Doo what we're on about. Most adults don't get it either. Which is why they're addicted to spending money to make themselves happy).

Yes, we know that a new computer game, iPod, laptop pair of shoes, etc will make you happy. But the happiness will quickly fade and you'll need to spend money again. If your happiness strategy is based on spending money it will always be short-lived. You need a better strategy: please keep reading.

Love your parents and always respect your elders. Your parents have done the best they could with what they know. We appreciate that it doesn't always appear this way. Put the book down now and go and give mum & step dad a cuddle. Go on, we dare you! And your gran too while you're at it. And your little brother. If they say 'what was that for?' say 'just because the little me in the clouds said I should.' And do it often.

They will think you're odd. Tell them you're not 'odd', you're 'extraordinary'. It's true.

Don't listen to your parents' advice about passion unless it's positive. If it's not positive, it's because they don't know what they are talking about. They grew up in a different time. If I listened to my Dad I would be working in a factory pulling feathers out of chickens' bums, waiting to retire in 30 years' time. #Nightmare!

Your passion won't knock on your door though, you have to go and find it. Lads, sitting at home spending hours on your X-Box might be cool when you're 15. It ain't cool when you're 38, especially if you're still living at home with your mum.

BTW, being a celebrity or 'famous' is not a passion. If you become famous it will be because of your passion and talent, but merely 'wanting to be famous' will hurt you. If your plan is to sit patiently and wait to be on Top Gear as the 'star in the reasonably priced car', the chances are you won't ever be on Top Gear and you won't be a star. 'Sitting patiently' is passive. You need to get off your backside and do something. But I don't want to quash your dreams entirely. The 'reasonably priced car' bit might be achievable?

Wanting to be famous is the same as wanting to be rich. If you really want to be famous, stop dreaming and do something awesome. You won't get rich without working your arse off.

I know, I know. There's a piece of you that's saying, 'I might win the lottery'. If your life strategy is based on winning the lottery, your life will be very sad indeed. Email me in 50 years and let me know how your strategy's going.[3]

TOP TIP

Cut down massively on TV, X-Box and social media. We're not saying cut it out completely. But less is better. While everyone else is Facebooking their life away you can be getting on with your secret long term ambition. That's what we did and it worked!

[3] True. We met a teenager whose life strategy was to win the lottery. He didn't need school. He certainly didn't need our advice. He was just going to spend his dole cheque on tickets. So far, he hasn't won. He's 38 and still lives in a one bed flat with his mum. He really needs our advice but is now too embarrassed to ask #terribleshame.

Success is always disguised as hard work. *Always, always, always!* That's why most people don't ever see it. It sometimes requires you to get up at 5am on cold, dark winter mornings when most people (especially teenagers) are still in bed. It's too much effort to get out of bed. It's too much effort to get out of bed early and do stuff. I mean, what's the point?

Exactly!

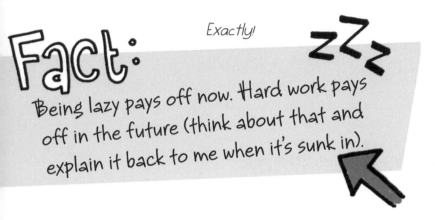

Fact:

Being lazy pays off now. Hard work pays off in the future (think about that and explain it back to me when it's sunk in).

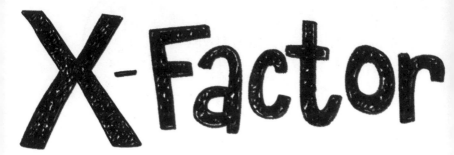

X-Factor

Which part of the X-factor do you enjoy most?

The auditions when the awful singers are on? Me too! Do you want the world to laugh at you, or with you?

If your plan is to find a rich partner and live off them, that is not finding your passion, that's being a WAG. It's also at the 'lottery win' end of the chance spectrum.

One of the best ways to create 'lasting' happiness in your life is to find your passion. Programmes like X-factor can help you like they helped Leona Lewis and Elvis. (I might be a bit behind the times?)

Massively reduce the odds of not being successful by studying hard or reading an awesome book (like this one) while everyone else watches telly. If you read 1 self-help book per week, that's 52 books a year, which is 1560 books in 30 years. That's a library! Holy cow, imagine how awesome you'd be?

Emotion creates motion. That means you are driven by your feelings.

Getting off your backside and being bothered about yourself creates opportunities. Not everyone takes the opportunities that come their way. Some people aren't ready. Some bottle it.

Be ready. Be prepared. And, most of all, be brave.
Say

'YES'

more than you say 'no'.

If you don't know what your passion is, that's OK. You need to start looking though, immediately. The sooner you find your passion the sooner your life will improve. Try the questions below and email us your answers. We'll give you marks out of 10 (yes, we really will!).

The Passion Finder

Under each question there is a gap. The gap isn't there because we were told the book had to be a bit longer by the publisher and we'd run out of things to say.
It is there so you can fill in answers as you think of them (probably?).

There is no right or wrong answer as far your passion is concerned.

1. What interests you now?

2. What interested you when you were younger?

3. What do you want?

4. What would make you happier?

5. Who are you at your best?

6. What milestones and events have been important in your life?

7. What achievements are you pleased about?

8. What 'less than happy' experiences have influenced you? What did you learn?

9. Write a list of things you feel good about in your life

10. What, for you, is 'success'?

11. Interviews with the elderly do not report that people have regret for the things they have done, but rather, people talk about the things they regret not having done. What are your thoughts on this?

_____
_____
_____
_____

12. What are the most important things life has taught you so far?

_____
_____
_____
_____

13. What are you capable of?

_____
_____
_____

14. It's your last day at school and teachers have written comments about you in a book. What would you like the comments to say?

_____
_____
_____
_____

We hope your brain is aching at this point. If it is - excellent! You're putting the right amount of effort in. If your brain isn't hurting please do the questions again because the final question is the biggest of the lot:

15. What have you learned from the activity above?

_____
_____
_____
_____

bonus Story

A young man was enrolling on the first day of his new university course. Stretching ahead was seven years of training that would eventually earn him a medical degree and the opportunity to work in the career he'd always wanted.

As he stood in the enrolment line he sparked up a conversation with an elderly gentleman standing behind him in the queue. Both men agreed that becoming a medic was something they've always dreamed of. The young man couldn't help commenting on the old man's age. 'If you don't mind me asking,' he enquired, 'how old are you?' 'I'm seventy-three,' beamed the old man.

The young man looked amazed. 'But that means that in seven years' time, when you qualify, you'll be eighty!'

The old man beamed again. 'Young fellow,' he said, 'in seven years' time I'll be eighty, whether I live my dream or not.'

Question: What do you understand this story to mean?

Earlier we said that when you find your 'why?' your rocket ship will be ready to launch. When a rocket takes off it uses 90% of its fuel getting off the launch pad. If you apply that analogy to people, we think it means you require a lot of energy to get started with something. Which is why we like the 4-minute rule.

It's deadly simple. Here it is. The first 4 minutes of any interaction are the most important.

If you can act like the best version of yourself for 4 minutes then it will have a significant impact on the people around you. In case you haven't twigged, your feelings are contagious. So positivity, enthusiasm and happiness are a bit like an awesome version of flu. We want you to infect people (in a nice way, of course).

The 4-minute rule generally starts by asking yourself a really cool question, 'What does the best version of me do for the next 4 minutes?' ... and then do it (even when you don't feel like it. In fact, especially when you don't feel like it).

You CAN do this ... but most people can't be bothered. If you can be bothered it can become an extremely powerful habit.

It has totally transformed Darrell's relationship with his kids. Here's a grown-up bit, but you'll be a grown-up one day (fingers crossed) so you might as well learn now.

Darrell's work involves him being away from home for a number of days. His two young sons would get really excited when he came home after not seeing them for a while.

'Sometimes I would be away for a whole week. The lads were allowed to stay up late on Friday to welcome me home. They were so excited they'd go bananas as I came through the door.

I wasn't excited though. I had driven for 3 hours on the motorway and all I wanted to do was get home, unpack my bags, get my jimjams on, have a cup of tea and go to bed - with the mission of being the best dad tomorrow after a good night's sleep. Maybe?

The OLD version of me did this:

I would walk in through the door and my two lads would come running to me, clinging to my legs, excitedly shouting, "Daddy, Daddy can we play cars?" (They loved playing a really simple game of racing cars on a road-mat placed on the floor.)

Picture me. Exhausted, crumpled, stressed. I ask you dear reader, do I look like I want to play effing cars? All I thought was "I've just been stuck in a car for 5 hours the last thing I wanted to do is play effing cars!"

So I would do the classic Dad "fob-off".
"Yeah, alright lads. Just let me get in the house and unpack my bags and I'll play cars with you in 15 minutes, ok?"

They would run off to get the road-mat and cars, shouting, "Mummy, mummy — daddy is going to play cars."

Tee, hee, hee. SUCKERS! Did I ever play cars? NOPE!

The "4-minute rule" has changed my life.

I now ask myself, "How would the best dad in the world go through that door?"

And the answer's obvious. Plus the great news is, I only have to do it for 4 minutes!

The NEW version of me forgets about my bags, jimjams and cuppa. It doesn't matter that I'm crumpled and exhausted. These are the most important people in my life so I burst through the door, dive on my sons and tell them we're playing cars. So, at first, I put a lot of effort into it. "You can be Lewis Hamilton, I'll be Jenson Button. Vroom, vroom."⁴

Sometimes I really don't feel like doing it and genuinely just want to go to bed, but after a couple of minutes I realise I'm enjoying myself. It's great father and son time. Why did I do the classic dad fob-off for so long?

Beware, enthusiasm is powerful stuff. If you do ever bother to play with any young relatives, you'll know that, after 4 minutes, you look up and they have cleared off, leaving you to it and making you look like a right idiot!
#VroomVroom

Here are a few situations for you to apply the 4-minute rule. How would the very best superhero version of you behave when:

You get home from school
You are walking into school
You have masses of homework
Maths is really tough
It's 7am and you're coming downstairs for breakfast
Your mum's nagging you to tidy your room

⁴ Darrell's kids are 24 and 21 #saddo.

CoMForT

Scientists have identified two types of young people. You can have a fixed or growth mind-set.

A fixed mind-set stops you doing things in a 'I'd better not try that in case I fail' kind of way. Hence, people with fixed mind-sets tend to exist well within their comfort zones. Life can pass them by while they stay safely and securely within their potential.

A growth mind-set is more expansive. We're summing up mightily but something like 'Life looks like a great adventure, let's give it a really good go.' The result is that they do things and stretch themselves. They tend to squeeze much more value out of their days.

Growth mind-set kids keep going, even when the going gets tough. Grit and determination may not be sexy, but they shine through.

Think of life as having two paths: one leading to mediocrity, the other to excellence. The path to mediocrity is temptingly flat and straight. Nice and easy. You can cruise along on autopilot with smooth and almost effortless progression.

The path to excellence couldn't be more different. It's like a mountain path in the Andes. The one that Jeremy Clarkson navigates in a Top Gear special. It's steep and gruelling with a sheer drop. It's longer too, requiring concentration and effort.

A growth mind-set is suited to this harder road. A fixed mind-set is perfect for the road to mediocrity. The spark that ignites you will be extinguished at the first sign of failure.

Here are some of the mind-set characteristics:
Growth mind-set:
Open to new ideas

Always learning (especially from setbacks)

Enjoy challenges

Believe that abilities develop

Believe that people and lives develop

Fixed mindset:
   Believe that ability and intelligence are born into you

Judgemental

Limit achievement (challenges scare you)

Believe that if a relationship needs work it must be wrong

Believe that if you have to work at things you must be
stupid. It should come naturally

I guess the obvious question is, which one are you?

And then there's what scientists call your 'explanatory
style'. Consider this scenario, you're on a plane, heading
on your jollies. You are strapped in, taxiing for take-off
and there's a faint whiff of smoke as the wheels leave
the tarmac. The plane climbs, circles once and the whiff
has turned into billowing black smoke. Panic ensues and
the pilot makes a very heavy landing. There are 200
people on board and all of them survive. There are a few
injuries and you are taken to hospital with a broken leg.

Something to ponder, Are you lucky or unlucky?

This kind of scenario links to your 'explanatory style' and
this has a crucial impact on your current and future
happiness.

An optimistic explanatory style interprets problems as local and temporary. ('It's only a broken leg, could have been an awful lot worse, and as soon as it's better I'll go on my hollies.')

A pessimistic style interprets problems as global and permanent. ('I've been seriously injured in a plane crash, it's a disaster, I will seek compensation because I can't ever fly again. It's holidays in Blackpool for ever more.')

As you can see, the belief generated by this event directly affects your actions. A permanent pessimistic outlook means things are bad and aren't likely to get any better so you sink into what scientists call 'learned helplessness'. This is when life can get very heavy indeed.

I appreciate that the emergency landing example is extreme. But you will have thousands of other incidents in your life that you are applying strategies to.

In terms of bouncing back from adversity, it's a matter of re-training yourself to have a more positive explanatory style. There's a saying something akin to 'it's never too late to have a brilliant childhood' which (we think?) means it's possible to reframe events in a way that you learn from them rather being traumatised by them.

I appreciate that it's not always easy. Have a quick go. Cast your mind back to a difficult time. What did you learn? How did you change? What in your life has changed for the better because of this? Is there anything about the difficult experience that you can, on reflection, be grateful for?

Life is a series of events. Then you have a chain of choices about those events which leads to more events. And your explanatory style can trap you in a never ending cycle of pain or free you into an upward spiral of pleasure and growth.

Yes, there are some big words and massive concepts in the previous sentence, so here it is again, a bit easier.

When the sun shines, it shines on everyone. When it rains, it rains on us all. At some point in their life, every single person will experience tragedy, failure, rejection, depression and hopelessness. Learning to bounce back is therefore very important.

The reasons for feeling negative about yourself are numerous. Growing up in a weird family. The criticism of an insensitive teacher. Comparing yourself to, and competing with, others. Being bullied. Being picked last at football. Blah blah blah.

I could eat a bowl of alphabet spaghetti and s✶✶✶ a better argument than that!

The reasons don't matter, they're history. What matters is now. This present moment. What you do going forward will make or break your life.

Paradox

The following is a paradox,

The next sentence is totally true

The sentence you just read is false

A paradox doesn't make sense consciously or logically. And life can feel exactly the same.

Some people will make lots of money. Each and every one of them will do it differently. There isn't a magical formula to make money.

There are libraries of personal development books aimed at older people. And diddly-squat for people of your age. I saw a homeless person reading our first book 'The Art of Being Brilliant' and obviously thought 'his life isn't brilliant.'

I then pondered the following questions

How do I know his life isn't brilliant?

What is a brilliant life?

Lots of people who have money are happy.

Lots of people who have money are unhappy.

Lots of poor people are happy.

Lots of poor people are unhappy.

Buying things will make you happy. For about an hour. But then you need to keep on buying things to maintain your happiness and before you know it you're applying online at Wonga and your life is over. Every advert on the TV is designed to make you unhappy with what you currently own.

Buy a better phone, then you'll be happy.

Buy these designer glasses. Then you'll be happy.

Switch to our bank, then you'll be happy.

Go to our fast food outlet, then you'll be happy.

We're certain that you'll be better off learning to be happy NOW. But that means you have to be less bothered by what other people have and learn to be satisfied with what you already own. And we appreciate that's a very tricky thing to learn to do.

Earlier we asked you to write a list of 10 things you appreciate but take for granted:

Keep this list by your bed. Look at it in the morning when you wake up. Look at what you already have! WowZa! Youth, education, a bed, mobile phone, life, your health, hot water, food, X-Box, a house, family, love, friends, a fridge, TV, wifi, sight, ears, functioning kidneys (tell me when you've got the point...) shoes, clothes, iPod, memories, Greggs, freedom, supermarkets, fresh air, trees, teachers, 250 TV channels, biscuits, clean pants, iPlayer, shampoo, Nandos, intelligence, nipples, Scotch eggs ...

Here's a thought - what if you've already got everything you actually need to be happy? What would happen if you focused on what you have got rather than moaning about what you haven't got? Like I say, just a thought.

What other people think of you is none of your business
Andrew Matthews
(author and happiness expert)

People

The media spends millions on using celebrities to promote their goods because they want you to believe if you buy their aftershave, clothes, cars etc. you will become like them or, at least for a few seconds of your life, feel like them.

It's a very powerful message. Back to an earlier top tip, be careful who you worship. Personally, I like the Beckhams. David and Victoria work extremely hard. We especially love the fact that they have called their children after the places they were conceived, 'Brooklyn' and 'Romeo'. I was telling my children 'Table top' and 'Back alley' all about them last night.

If you want to experience the kind of success the Beckham's have don't worry about what they are wearing and driving, but do take inspiration from the fact they have worked their socks off, followed their dreams and cared about other people. Don't look up to them, look into them.

Here comes another paradox 'if you want people to care about you, you have to care more about them.'

I bet you know someone who all they want to do is talk about themselves 'Check me out, my new clothes, my new bag, my new face!' You listen for a while but it gets annoying.

My NEW Bag My NEW Clothes Blah Blah Blah its all about ME!

I bet you also know someone who just listens to you and genuinely takes an interest in what you have been doing.

Who do you prefer spending time with?

I'm guessing it's the listener.

You need to be that person.

Always do what you say you will do. In short, keep your word and (to the best of your ability) never let people down.

Give people compliments. Catch them doing things well, and tell them. Speak highly of people. In fact, speak highly of people behind their back. It's another of those spooky things that pays back a million times over during your lifetime. Technically it's called 'spontaneous trait transference'. We don't want to bog you down with big words so we'll gloss over it. If you're interested (which we hope you will be), Google it.

Always we hear the cry from teenagers, "where can we go, what can we do?" My answer is this: go home, mow the lawn, wash the windows, learn to cook, build a raft, get a job, visit the sick, study your lessons and after you've finished, read a book. Your town does not owe you recreational facilities and your parents do not owe you fun. The world does not owe you a living. You owe the world something. You owe it your time, energy and talent...in other words, grow-up, stop being a cry baby, get out of your dream world and develop a backbone instead of a wishbone. Start behaving like a responsible person. You are important and you are needed. It's too late to sit around and wait for somebody to do something, someday. Someday is now and that somebody is you.

John Tepene
(head teacher
from New Zealand)

Impact

A   B   C   D

Multiple choice time. Just like school! In the previous quote what is John really talking about?

A. Mowing the lawn
B. Building rafts
C. Earning extra pocket money by helping with a few chores
D. The fact that coming alive, NOW, is the key to your future. The world needs you to be your best self, right now. Start taking personal responsibility for your life. Quit moaning about stuff and pull your finger out. Quit sitting around waiting for life to take off. Put the effort into launching yourself. RIGHT NOW!

Yes, you're absolutely right. The answer is B. Global warming is coming your way so raft-building is very important. Learn now, before it's too late. You could become the new Noah.

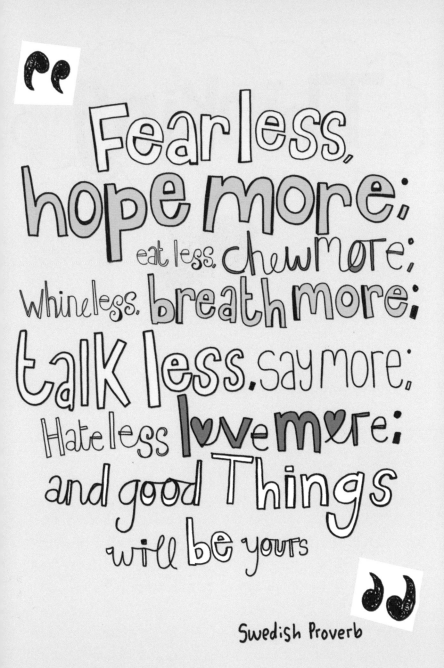

Fear less,
hope more;
eat less, chew more;
whine less, breath more;
talk less, say more;
Hate less love more;
and good Things
will be yours

Swedish Proverb

Here's another multi-choice: Who taught you how to think?

A. Your mum
B. Your grandma
C. Society
D. Monkeys
E. Nobody

At school you have lessons which teach you about stuff, reading, writing, algebra, how to make spag bol, Hitler, ox-bow lakes, Newton's laws of motion, tectonic plates and how to ask for directions to the toilet in Paris. *Oui?*

And although thinking helped you get the answers to all of these, you never had thinking lessons. Nobody ever sat you down and said, *Righty ho, this is how you need to*

think in order to have a fabulous life.' Or at least, that
never happened in my school.

So, if nobody actually taught you how to think ... where
did your thinking come from?

The short answer is ... you made it up! When you were
growing up you looked at the people around you and
they had a way of thinking and behaving that you copied.
You desperately wanted to fit in. And the best way to fit
in is to think and behave just like everyone else.

And that's absolutely fine. So long as you want to be
like everybody else? But we're pitching this book in at the
brilliant end of the spectrum. We don't want you to be
like everybody else (because, as we said earlier, that'd
make you 'average').

So, here's a hairy monster of a question, think of all the
thinking you've ever done and dare to ask yourself, what
if there was a better way?

And here's the hairy monster of an answer.

THERE IS!

I was in Sainsbury's. To be exact I was in the fruit and vegetable section admiring the broccoli. Strictly speaking I wasn't admiring it, I was wondering why some broccoli had plastic wrapped around it and other bits of broccoli didn't. Why should some broccoli be free to breathe and feel the world against its cool green exterior and other broccoli be confined to a plastic cell? I obviously had far too much time on my hands.

I'm sure you have had the experience of being in a crowded place and you just get this sixth sense feeling that someone is looking at you. I looked up. A lady was staring at me. I felt I knew her from somewhere but I'm rubbish with faces and names so I chose my broccoli (no plastic, I like my broccoli to be alive when I plunge it into the boiling water) and moved on.

Yoghurt. So much choice! I looked up from the Muller Fruit Corners and there was the lady again. Still staring at me! How rude! She cast a weak smile my way. My mind clicked through its stored images. Mel? Could it really be Mel from school? After 30 years?

The lady was walking towards me, holding her arms out for a cuddle. If I'm honest she looked like she had eaten Mel from school (you do tend to put a bit of weight on as you get older).

She mouthed, 'Are you Andy?'

'Yes,' I nodded and we started running towards each other like the long lost lovers that we never were. We met in a big hug at the breakfast cereals, my arms failing to get all the way around Mel.

'Gosh, is it you?' I asked, noticing the Honey Monster on the sugar puffs packet in her basket. I knew that people looked like their dogs and all of a sudden I wondered if they also ended up looking like their breakfast cereals? I made a mental note not to mention this to Mel.

'It iiiiis,' she squealed, her face reddening a little. 'It's meeee. I saw you earlier. You know, next to the broccoli. And I thought it might be you Andy.'

I was delighted to see her. 'It must be 30 years?' I said, a huge grin lighting up my mush.

'32,' stated Mel proudly. 'I haven't seen you for 32 years. Not since we left school.'

'Holy cow,' I said, regretting the choice of phrase. I was so thrilled to meet an old school chum after 32 years, especially so randomly, at the supermarket. 'Mel,' I said, 'how have your 32 years been?'

And Mel rolled her eyes and sighed a huge sigh. 'Andy,' she said, 'they've been booooring.'

Know what? I've got a real problem with that story. My problem?

It's true!

And it highlights the painful reality that has been the undercurrent of the entire book. The habits that you get into now will stick with you for the rest of your life. Remember, Melanie was booooring in year 4 and she's booooooring at age 44. Therefore, if you get into good habits NOW, those good habits will also stick with you forever. It's not too late guys and gals.

Little things like turning up to school with a great attitude. If you like learning now, you'll like learning later.

Like turning off the TV and reading a chapter of a book. If you get into reading now, you'll like reading later.

Like having a great attitude and trying your hardest. Because if you have a great attitude and try hard now ... you'll prosper later.

Do your homework first time of asking. To a very high standard.

Use your manners.

Manage your time wisely.

Be a great friend.

Eat healthily.

Get fit.

Be positive.

Talk to yourself nicely.

Play to your strengths.

#nuffsaid

"I don't want to get to the end of my life and find that I just lived the length of it. I want to have lived the width of it as well."

Diane Ackerman
(American author and poet)

Phone a Friend

RING

CALLING A FRIEND

RING

Now, I know this may be scary for you, but actually seeking, finding and then asking someone for advice is something only stupid people DON'T do!

WARNING! Make sure you ask the right advice to the right person. If you want to be a pilot, don't ask Will.i.Am. He may be a great music producer but I doubt he can fly a 747 any better than us.

Fact:

There are thousands of other young people your age who also want the same career as you.

What could you do that gives you the edge?

Here is a simple process you can do in a matter of minutes (which a lot of young people can't be bothered to do) - so put your mobile phone down and spend the next 10 minutes doing the following.

Search online to find out what type of jobs/careers utilise your favourite skills.

Contact these companies/people via email, asking for advice.

(Act on the advice when it comes).

Right ... back to your mobile, no doubt you've missed an important Facebook update from a friend who has amazingly taken a picture of a baked bean they had for tea which looks nothing like a famous popstar though they reckon it does.

Go a step further.

Search for the world's best person in your chosen career.

Contact them for advice.

Ask them if you can keep them up-to-date with your progress.

Scared? What's the worst thing that could happen?? They say 'up yours you spotty faced teenager'. So what? You will have learnt another one of life's lessons 'Some people, sometimes are not very nice.'

Whether you get a reply or not from the world's best people (and the more people you contact the more chance you'll have of getting advice - some of which could be potentially awesome for your life), you still also need to get a mentor a bit closer to home.

Within your circle of friends, family, year group at school and even teachers, it's likely they will know someone that it would be useful for you to meet - so ask.

If this circle of people can't help, then do it yourself.

If you want to be a nurse, then ask to speak to one at your local GP surgery.

If you want to be a mechanic, then get your ass to a garage.

If you want to fit tyres, contact my mate Mark Lichfield at BM Motors in Mansfield. (He buys me a drink for every referral from the book. Lesson? Always have more than one revenue stream).

You will be amazed at how many adults are out there, who are more than happy to be able to help out someone like you, if you only ask in an energetic and positive way.

Bouncebackability

While we want this book to make you feel good about yourself, it will absolutely and definitely not make your life go smoothly. Life is less like an ocean cruise and more like white water rafting.

So when things do go wrong, here are a couple of questions to ask yourself to help you bounce back (thanks to Paul McGee).

Where is this issue on a scale of 1 to 10? (1 is insignificant, 10 is death.)

How important will this be in 12 months' time?

If you come to the conclusion that the issue is a 3 or below, you won't even remember anything about it in two weeks' time, let alone a year's time. So we suggest you stop moaning about it and crack on with your life. If it's a 7 or higher, and you are convinced this will be burned into your brain for life, then can we suggest you stop moaning about it and take some form of action to get it sorted.

Ask yourself - what does the best version of me do to solve this ... and then do it.

Future

You may know people who moan about their job. They wake up on Monday and all they are thinking about is getting to Friday and then waiting to retire. My Dad's generation had a job for life, people walked out of school with no qualifications and straight into a menial job, usually in a factory. This world doesn't exist anymore.

Sure there are still people finishing off their time in organisations (usually moaning about the fact their pension isn't going to pay out what it should). Not only is your world very different to that of your parents, it's going to keep changing at what your grandparents would describe as 'an alarming rate.'

I know someone, of an older generation, who maintains that 'work isn't something you enjoy, it's just something you have to do'. Life can be like that but it doesn't have to be.

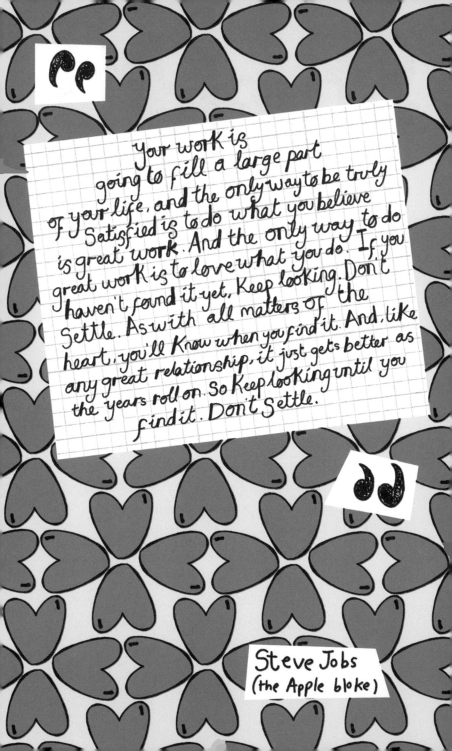

" Your work is going to fill a large part of your life, and the only way to be truly satisfied is to do what you believe is great work. And the only way to do great work is to love what you do. If you haven't found it yet, keep looking. Don't settle. As with all matters of the heart, you'll know when you find it. And, like any great relationship, it just gets better as the years roll on. So keep looking until you find it. Don't settle. "

Steve Jobs
(the Apple bloke)

Stupidity

This chapter tells it as it is, no punches pulled.

Fact:

A common mistake that people make when trying to design something completely fool-proof is to underestimate the ingenuity of complete fools.

We have just finished an afternoon with around 90 students who had just finished year 11 and were going on to 6th form. They've got the grades. The 6th form choice is purely theirs. Nobody is forcing them. It's a free world. Most of them were great, but there were a handful (mainly lads on the same table) who you would be forgiven for thinking were dick-heads. We appreciate that isn't perhaps the kindest term and we considered toning it down. Maybe they were just having a bad day? Maybe they had a horrible home life? Maybe they were misunderstood? Maybe it wasn't their fault that they treated us with a complete lack of respect?

But dear reader, there's no ducking this fact - there are dick-heads in every school. Rich ones, poor ones, brown, white, black, male, female, thin, fat, brainy, not-so-brainy, sporty, not-so-sporty, geeky, gay, spotty, trendy, goth ... and, ultimately, there are no excuses. As you get older, you don't really change. You become more and more of who you already are.

Fact:

Every teenager is dripping with potential but not every teenager will fulfil their potential. Some will completely waste it and end up living a pale shadow of the life they could have had. Your challenge is to not become one. Or, if you already have the tendencies, to change before it's too late.

Let's tell you about our afternoon. Isn't it strange how all the 'cool' ones get together, no doubt all convincing themselves that the right thing to do is ignore us and muck around instead.
We asked everyone to discuss,

'What is the biggest thing that can transform your upcoming year 12 from being "OK" to being "awesome"?'
This is how the discussion went on the problem table:

Us: 'So what do you think it is?'

Problem lad 1: 'Red-stripe?'

All problem lads together: (Laughter)

Problem lad 2: 'Kopparberg'?

All problem lads together: (Laughter)

Problem lad 3: 'Stella?'

All problem-lads together: (Laughter)
(Note, same gag 3 times and still laughing? Never a good sign.)

We had a quiet word. We explained the difference between someone who was 'an idiot' and someone who was 'stupid'. 'An idiot' we said is when people are so thick that they can't understand what we're on about. Whereas 'stupid' is when they do understand but don't do it. We asked them which they were.

Cue a little confusion before they proudly admitted they were 'stupid'. *'We get it sir, we're just too cool to be bothered.'*

And that's fine. We turned our attention to those who who could be bothered. Because, you see, we can't do much about stupidity. We desperately wanted the lads to 'get it'. To understand that if they applied the principles to their lives, their lives would be full colour 3D HD instead of black & white.

But it's not good enough US wanting their lives to be awesome. Sadly, they have to want it too. And we come full circle. It's easier to be stupid.

And, grudgingly, we kind of agree that it can be 'cool' to mess around and be one of the crowd. Or, to clarify that comment, it's cool if you're 14 or 15.

It's not so cool 20 years later when you're in a bedsit eating beans that were warmed on a camping stove. In fact, I promise you that's very 'uncool' indeed.

Please note, this kind of story also applies to teenage girls. Lack of confidence is often masked by an instinctive yelp of 'I don't get it, sir,' when they're asked a question in class. Occasionally we are hit with a steadfast, unshakable negative attitude and a shrug of the shoulders. Girls can be the worst.

Interestingly, we got to chat to one of the lads about his potential goal in life. As he was a decent distance away from his mates, he was totally different. He seemed to be genuinely worried about not knowing what he wanted to do. He seemed a bit fidgety. The camping stove thing was lurking in his mind. And, on a one to one level, he seemed really engaged.

So, here's a curious thing, he was only stupid when he was in a crowd. Same with the difficult girls. How odd.

So, a quick reminder of a crucial message a couple of paragraphs ago - *you don't really change, you become more and more of who you already are.*

In which case it's definitely worth being confident, positive, upbeat, hard-working, happy and stand-out awesome.

NOW

Because becoming more and more of that kind of person is the key to the rest of your life. Back to that little version of you perched up on the cloud. They're watching and advising. What would they tell you to do?

The SCHOOL Reunion

20 years from now you are going to meet up with your whole school year for a night of catching up, reflection and sharing what you have achieved in your life.

How old will you be in 20 years? Now imagine that you are that age. Write 2 pages that reflect on your 20 years

Page 1: Imagine you've coasted for 20 years. You dossed at school and wasted your time. Basically, you couldn't really be bothered. How has your life turned out? What job are you doing? Who are you with? What do you own? How do you feel? What do people say about you?

Page 2: Imagine you've been awesome for 20 years. You knuckled down at school and had a superb attitude. How has your life turned out? What job are you doing? Who are you with? What do you own? How do you feel? What do people say about you?

Compare your potential lives. Choose the best one and live it.

bonus activity

We'd like to read these. 'Brilliant' teeshirts for the best ones.

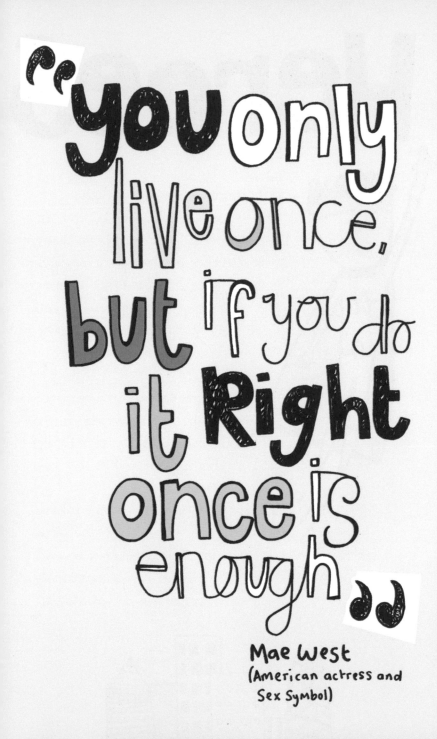

"you only live once, but if you do it right once is enough"

Mae West
(American actress and Sex Symbol)

Heroes

Everyone needs heroes. Make sure you worship the right kind of heroes. I feel the pendulum might have swung towards celebrity for the sake of itself. For 'hero' read 'celebrity'. And for 'celebrity' read 'vacuous orange person with boob job and collagen lips, from a reality show, probably in Essex'.

This book isn't about what you want to be. The subliminal question throughout has been, 'what kind of person do you want to be.'

Let me remind you that the average lifespan in the UK is about 4000 weeks. I want you to be a superhero for however many of those weeks you've got left. Not the vacuous reality-TV kind of hero, more the jaw-dropping 'made of positive stuff' kind.

'Go-Getter Girl', a hero to her children and grandchildren. A shining light to her work colleagues and a beacon of positivity to whomever she meets. You need to say that in a deep movie-trailer voice. It has a nice ring to it.

But, of course, being a superhero takes a bit of effort. It's a lot easier to be ...

'Bog-Standard Man', striving for mediocrity and the weekends, living a luke-warm life and spreading averageness wherever he goes. Even with the voice that doesn't sound nearly as good.

And the truth is that we can't do it for you. The most important point is that you need to want to be a super-hero too!

'How we spend our days,' Annie Dillard once wrote, is, of course, 'how we spend our lives.' Our lives are a chain of these days. We grow, or we stagnate. We can form good habits or destructive ones. Or, more often than not, both. We learn from our mistakes, or we keep repeating them until we're in enough pain to make changes.

He stared at the gorgeous country whilst leaning against the door of his car. He had some important decisions to make. His smart-phone was making him stupid: that was for sure. His satnav was causing him to lose his sense of direction. His microwave was removing his love of food. E-mail was damaging good relationships. Box-sets were wrecking his love-life. And the heated drivers seat was making him soft.

Nicholas Bate
(British author and creative thinker)

I can think back through my years and trace a path to where I am now. But there is no straight arrow pointing from 'teenager with greasy hair and denim jacket' to 'middle-aged man tapping away at laptop'.

Life isn't a simple game of dot-to-dot. I doubt you have a plan. I'm not absolutely sure that I have? Life isn't as smooth as 'A leads to B and then to C … and you die at Z.'

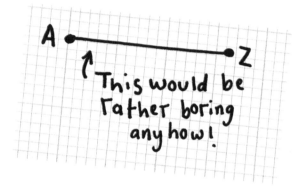

Life is a scribbly, scrawl of a line. It can look a right mess!

But if I could reach back through time and whisper something to that denim-clad youth with the poster of the bare-bottomed tennis lady on his bedroom wall, it would simply be this:

Be patient. Be positive. And effing wake up.

Funny rating 7.5
Clever rating 9.3
Fave quote: 'If you think education is expensive, try ignorance.'

Curing misery

Dr HAPPY

Andy C: Clever guy who spends 50% of his time as a student, 50% as an author and 50% as a trainer (not so clever at maths, to be fair). Andy works with massive companies, reminding them how to be happy. He also writes the 'Spy Dog' children's series. One daughter, one son.

Funny Bone

Andy W: Funny guy who has several failed careers before finding his niche - delivering training that makes people laugh as well as changing their lives. Fluctuates between genius and idiot. One daughter.

Creating smiles wherever he goes

Funny rating 9.9
Clever rating 1.4
Fave quote: 'The past, the present and the future walked into a bar. It was tense.'

Arty-Amy

Amy: Fun girl who gets to spend her days doing her favourite thing...DRAWING!! She's always saying she has the best job!! If you'd like to see more of her cool illustrations then visit www.amybradley.co.uk

Funny rating 7.7
Clever rating 7.2
Fave quote:
'If you have good thoughts, they will shine out of your face like sunbeams and you will always look lovely.'

Creating pictures to brighten your life

- Mr Strengths -

Daz: Nice guy who had a successful career in local radio before deciding to jack it all in and do something radical with his life. He now delivers 'The Art of Being Brilliant' in business and schools. Two sons.

Funny rating 7.5
Clever rating 9.1
Fave quote:
'When one door closes, it's shut.'

Finding your inner power